Montessori at Home Guide

A SHORT PRACTICAL MODEL TO GENTLY
GUIDE YOUR 2 TO 6-YEAR-OLD THROUGH
LEARNING SELF-CARE

Rachel Peachey

Cover art by: Robert McKinney

Sterling Production
LEXINGTON, KENTUCKY

Copyright © 2016 by A. M. Sterling

All rights reserved. No part of this publication may be reproduced, distributed or transmitted in any form or by any means, including photocopying, recording, or other electronic or mechanical methods, without the prior written permission of the publisher, except in the case of brief quotations embodied in critical reviews and certain other noncommercial uses permitted by copyright law. For permission requests, write to the publisher, addressed "Attention: Permissions Coordinator," at the address below.

Sterling Production
www.sterlingproduction.com
ashleyandmitch@sterlingproduction.com

Montessori at Home Guide: A Short Practical Model to Gently Guide Your 2 to 6-Year-Old Through Learning Self-Care

Rachel Peachey – 1st ed.
ISBN-13: 978-1539419266
SBN-10: 1539419266

Contents

Potty Learning 18

Wiping After Using the Bathroom 21

Brushing Teeth 22

Washing Hands.. 23

Taking A Bath 26

Taking a Shower 27

Washing the Face 28

Combing Hair 29

Blowing the Nose.. 30

Sneezing/Coughing into Elbow 31

Applying Lotion... 32

Clipping Nails... 32

Dressing Frames 37

Putting Clothes in the Laundry Basket 39

Putting on Shoes and Rain Boots 39

Putting on a Jacket 40

Putting on Pants 41

Putting on a Hat 42

Putting on Socks 42

Putting on a Belt 42

Folding Clothes 43

Hanging Up Clothes 44

Choosing Appropriate Clothing 45

Making the Bed 45

Sewing a Button 46

How to Use an Umbrella 47

Chewing and Swallowing Food 52

Drinking from a Cup 52

Using Utensils 53

Using a Napkin at Mealtime 53

Pouring a Drink 54

Serving a Snack 54

Applying Sunscreen 60

Applying Bug Repellent 61

Knowing Parent's Names 61

Learning Last Names 62

Learning the Address... 62

Learning Phone Numbers 63

Awareness of Surroundings 64

Reading Basic Signs 64

Learning to Call 911 64

Basic First Aid 65

Fire Safety 66

Strangers and Other Dangers 67

Traffic Lights and Pedestrian Indicators..................... 68

Identifying First Responders and Helpers 68

What to Do in a Tornado 69

Calming Down 72

Being Thankful 73

Saying "Please" 74

Saying "Sorry" 74

Resolving Conflict 75

Being Silent 75

    Resources 79

    About the Author 81

    About the Publishers 83

"Children are human beings to whom respect is due, superior to us by reason of their innocence and of the greater possibilities of their future."
- DR. MARIA MONTESSORI

Chapter One

Introduction

Whether you are a parent, caretaker or educator, you are concerned for the well-being of the young children in your care. The exciting and fascinating time from ages 2-6 marks an amazing period of changes and milestones reached. Children change from toddling, unstable, barely communicative little ones into running, jumping, climbing and expressive beings.

One of the main focal points for children during this time is independence. Every inch of their little bodies pushes them to do things "all by myself." With the help of the Montessori method, many parents, caregivers and educators have fostered and validated this need, guiding children to develop many skills that increase their independence.

This book provides some direction for those wishing to teach the important skills of self-care. Each of the tasks outlined here increase the child's sense of independence, and through this, her confidence. Though activities focusing on learning to dress, feed and manage hygiene may seem mundane to us adults, for children, mastering these skills is a ticket to freedom. Imagine what it would be like to need to ask for help every time you wanted a glass of water or to put your shoes on. You would be dependent on another person's availability constantly!

Many times, parents, caregivers and educators alike perform many of these self-care tasks for the child in an effort to help them.

However, by giving the child the chance to do these things on her own, we allow her to develop her own sense of self, her independence and her need to have some control in her life.

As you use this guide, try to step back and give your child some space. It may take some time for you to eliminate the urge you feel to swoop in and help your child. However, if your child is not frustrated or discouraged, chances are she doesn't need any help at all! As adults, we are often in a hurry and wish to see tasks completed quickly. Whenever possible, give your child additional time. Remember, they are learning new skills and mastering fine motor control. They are working.

Also, remember that each child is unique. While some two-year-olds are quick to learn to use the potty, other children aren't ready until they are nearly three. Some children may prefer food related activities to dressing activities. Notice the areas where your child seems most engaged and focus on these topics first.

Allow your child to move at her own pace. Although it can be tempting to compare your child's abilities with those of other children, this often isn't helpful for you or your child. Each child has different interests and strengths. With patience, time and taking care to notice your child's interests, she'll have mastered most of the skills discussed in this guide before you know it.

We hope you find this book to be a helpful resource to guide you in how to begin teaching self-care to your young child. There's little in life more satisfying than observing the feeling of satisfaction on a child's face when mastering a new skill. Enjoy the journey!

"Never help a child with a task at which he feels he can succeed."
- DR. MARIA MONTESSORI

CHAPTER TWO

A Short History of the Montessori Method

Dr. Maria Montessori is the amazing woman behind the Montessori Method. Her unique observations made over a century ago are still relevant and revolutionary today. She was an extraordinary visionary who still offers lessons in the understanding of human development, particularly in understanding the youngest of children.

Montessori was trained as a doctor in Italy, her native country. Shortly after graduation in 1896, she took an interest to psychology and spent time working with children who were considered mentally ill. During this time, she studied and was inspired by other great thinkers of the time such as Edouard Seguin and Jean Marc Gaspard Itard.

Montessori created the beginnings of what would become her method while working with poor children in a ghetto of Rome. Hired to take care of factory worker's children by a group of investors, her curiosity and love for children led her to do much more than look after them. She called the project "Casa dei Bambini." It was here, through careful observation of the children and employment of methods typically reserved for mentally retarded children, that she began developing her teaching style. Using only the help of a few cleaning ladies, she managed a large group of children. She also created her own learning materials such as beads for counting, wooden letters, specially designed blocks and many, many others. Throughout her time there, she discovered a number of important things about children including:

- Children prefer to work with real objects and materials, not toys.
- Children do best without external rewards.
- Children enjoy having control over their environment. Appropriately sized furniture and the tools for cleaning are necessary in a Montessori environment.
- Interaction between younger and older children adds a wonderful richness to the learning environment with many benefits.
- The role of the teacher is that of a guide.
- Children require freedom of movement.
- Children are naturally interested in mastering certain activities and topics when provided with the appropriate guidance, materials and opportunities.
- For a child to learn and discover to her full potential, the teacher must "follow" her. Children show in their actions and interests what they want to learn. It is the teacher's job to cultivate and develop the child's abilities based on her interests.
- Children require time to work individually without interruption.
- Children are not empty vessels to be filled, but complete beings who only require freedom, guidance and the opportunity to discover the world around them.
- Young children learn by imitation.

Her methods quickly became popular and famous around the world. Today, the Montessori Method is still very popular both in the school and homeschool setting. Her teachings offer more than lesson plans and curriculum. It is a way of life, a way of interacting with children that promotes respect and a joy of learning.

Montessori's methodology is one of the only ones to place a focus on self-care. Her unique, well-rounded curriculum includes the development of the whole person. Montessori believed that one of the main goals for 2-6 year olds is independence. Thus, she argued that for a child to master her environment, she must be taught to care for herself. In the curriculum, this area of self-care falls under "practical life". This area focuses on the development of independence and coordination of movement that young children must master.

In the Montessori curriculum, there are a great many activities that belong to the practical life area. This guide focuses specifically on the self-care area of practical life in which children learn to maintain their appearance, manage their hygiene in a socially acceptable way, how to manage mealtime, how to dress and topics related to safety.

"These words reveal the child's inner needs: 'Help me to do it myself.'"
- DR. MARIA MONTESSORI

CHAPTER THREE

Hygiene

Have you ever noticed how young children are experts at getting dirty? Wiping boogers across their faces, submerging their hands into mud, dirt and any unclean surface, their curiosity often results in quite a mess. However, children also have a desire to become independent and manage their own hygiene. Ultimately, they'd like to learn the socially acceptable ways to handle themselves when it comes to cleanliness and enjoy engaging in these activities when they are taught.

One of the most important elements in hygiene is independence. A child who can easily wash his or her own hands has no need to interrupt or depend on an adult. Similarly, being able to blow their own nose helps children develop greater awareness of their body and needs.

This chapter will cover a number of hygiene related tasks that children can learn and master between the ages of 2 and 6. Below is a list of the lessons included in this chapter:

- Potty learning
- Wiping after using the bathroom
- Brushing teeth
- Washing hands
- Taking a bath
- Taking a shower
- Washing the face

- Combing hair
- Blowing the nose
- Sneezing/coughing into elbow
- Applying lotion
- Clipping nails

Each of the lessons are outlined with helpful pointers as to how you may present them to the child in your care.

Potty Learning

While some children are already potty trained by age 2, the majority are still working on this skill or have yet to begin potty learning. Most children develop interest in using the toilet on their own. As parents and caregivers, we must ensure that the necessary steps are taken so the child can follow this interest, become aware of his or her body, bowels and bladder, and begin to use the toilet.

The term "potty learning" is used because potty training focuses more on the parent or caregiver's role. However, this skill, as with every skill mastered, should focus on the child's learning process and interest. Potty learning shifts the action more into the child's domain. This can greatly help us as parents and caregivers, as we are reminded that we don't get to decide the timeline or exert pressure. With the right tools and opportunities, children can master potty skills, just as they do many other skills including walking and talking.

Children must be both physically and emotionally prepared to use the toilet. Physically, children must be able to control their bowels and bladder. This happens through the development of the nervous system. As the nervous system becomes ever more integrated through myelination, toddlers gain more exact control over their movements, including over sphincter muscles that control the bladder and bowels. By around 18 months, this process is completed in most children.

Potty learning also involves a child's interests and desires to grow in his or her independence and to copy their parents and older siblings if they have them. From as young as a year old, some babies show interest in following their parents to the bathroom and watching how they use the toilet. It's best to encourage this interest if possible, as it will help the child when beginning to use the toilet on their own.

Another helpful practice is the use of cloth diapers. With cloth diapers, children can more easily feel when they have urinated. This allows the child to connect the feeling in their bladder and the wetness, developing a greater awareness of their body that will help them know when they need to use the potty.

To begin more formal potty learning, caregivers can help their children by making a potty chair available. Some people experience greater success by moving the chair to the bedroom or another area of the house that's comfortable for the child. It's also advisable to encourage your child to wear underwear rather than diapers. Even though it's likely that accidents will still happen, the results will be more obvious. Children can help clean up accidents with old towels. Consider keeping clean underwear and towels in an easily accessible location so that your child can grab them after an accident. A hamper can also be provided for wet and dirty items.

Reassurance and calmness surrounding accidents is essential. Both parents and caregivers must take a matter-of-fact approach surrounding accidents so that the child doesn't associate the learning process with negative experiences. Similarly, encouragement should be given for children when using the potty correctly. Rather than showering the child in praise, caregivers can focus on the benefits of using the toilet. For example: "It's great you used the potty! Now you don't need diapers."

Many parents have success with a variety of techniques to make the potty chair and potty learning easier. For example, some use dolls or stuffed animals, pretending they use the potty. This can help make the potty chair seem more normal. Others remove impediments such as underpants completely, allowing the child to move about the home bottomless as they become accustomed to using the potty.

Even when children become quite skilled at using the potty during the daytime, a diaper may still be needed at night. Over time, your child will learn to use the toilet at night time as well. One tactic to help during this stage is to take your child to the toilet after they've been asleep for an hour, and putting them back to bed after they've urinated.

Finally, young children are prone to accidents. It's best not to make a big deal out of them. Remember, your child is learning to recognize the sensation of the need to use the toilet. When distracted or excited, he or she may even avoid going to the toilet so as not to miss out on an activity. In the early stages of potty learning, ask your child if they need to go to the potty frequently. When going out, take an extra set of pants and underwear to avoid embarrassment and a sense of helplessness should an accident occur. As your child becomes more and more skilled at using the potty, you'll no longer need to remind them or carry extra clothing.

Potty learning is an exciting time of independence and achievement for your child. Try to look at it as a long process that will be achieved slowly, and at your child's pace. Your patience and encouragement will help your child succeed as he or she learns this important skill.

Wiping After Using the Bathroom

Although potty learning may be complete, your child will likely still need assistance to use toilet paper for wiping after using the bathroom.

The Montessori teaching method promotes modeling, guided practice and independent practice. The same approach can be taken when teaching this skill. See the steps below:

1. Modeling. If you're comfortable, allowing your child in the bathroom when you go can be a very easy and clear way of showing how to wipe after using the bathroom. However, if you prefer greater privacy, you may make a point of showing your child how you wipe them and each step you take.

2. Toilet Paper. You may consider practicing this when there's no need to use the potty. This way, you'll have your child's full attention, not worrying about anything else going on such as just having used the toilet, etc. Show your child how you pull the toilet paper off the roll and wrap or fold it up. Ask your child "Would you like to try?" Allow your child to try. If any changes are necessary, show your child the process again, and then allow them to try again. You needn't use a lot of words. Let your actions do the teaching. You can save the pieces of toilet paper to be used later.

3. Wiping. When it comes to wiping, show them how to hold the toilet paper and wipe their bottom. For girls, it's important to teach them to wipe from front to back to avoid contamination that could result in an infection. Then, you'll want to tell them to get clean toilet paper and wipe again, repeating until the toilet paper shows up clean.

4. Guided Practice. It's wise to accompany your child to the bathroom, especially for number 2, for a few weeks to ensure

they are using proper wiping habits. Talk together about how much toilet paper to use and how to tell when they have wiped enough.

5. Independent Practice. When you and your child feel ready, allow your child to complete this bathroom skill on their own. If you notice stained underwear or your child complains about an itchy bottom, it may be time for a refresher. Your child may be rushing, or needs more practice wiping properly. Take the time to ask your child if they remember how to wipe properly and remind them to take their time.

If your child seems reluctant to do the wiping on their own, ask your child if they can remember the steps. Talk your child through the process and be as encouraging as possible. Before you know it, your child will be able to perform all bathroom related skills on his or her own!

Brushing Teeth

Because young children enjoy doing what their parents do and copying them, by the age of two, your child has likely shown interest in brushing his or her teeth. This is an easy and fun skill to teach.

Begin by setting out all of the materials that will be needed on your counter: two toothbrushes (yours and your child's), toothpaste, a cup and a towel. Ensure that your child can reach the sink easily. Provide a step stool if necessary. Show your child each step, inviting them to repeat after you.

1. Put a small amount of toothpaste on your toothbrush. Ask your child if he/she would like to try. You may need to assist with squeezing the tube so that the right amount is used.

2. Brush teeth. Show your child how you brush all of your teeth, the top row and bottom, front teeth and back teeth, outside and inside. Invite your child to brush with you.
3. Spit. Show your child how you spit the toothpaste into the sink.
4. Rinse. Using the cup, take a little bit of water into your mouth and then spit it into the sink. Ask your child to repeat.
5. Rinse your toothbrush under the tap. Ask your child to try.
6. Wipe your hands and face with the towel. Ask your child to do the same.

For the first few times your child brushes his or her teeth, ensure that very little toothpaste is used to avoid complications from swallowing. While a little bit of toothpaste is not dangerous, regularly swallowing a large amount of toothpaste is not advisable.

As an extension or for further practice, you may want to use a dental teaching model (fake teeth) with your child. Show your child how to brush all of the teeth carefully using toothpaste, and then rinse them off.

Washing Hands

Hand washing is a daily experience for most young children. Two lessons have been included. One shows why hand washing is important and the second lesson teaches independent hand washing.

Why We Wash Hands

For this activity, it's best if your child has done something quite messy beforehand such as eating, helping in the garden, or similar.

Before presenting this lesson, gather your materials. You'll need: a pitcher with water, a bar of soap, a large bowl and a towel. Arrange these items on a table in the same order as listed, from left to right.

1. Tell your child, "Today we're going to learn why we need to wash our hands."
2. Ask your child to place their hands over the bowl. Pour some water over their hands.
3. Ask your child to use some soap and scrub their hands over the bowl. Ensure that your child's hands are well scrubbed and bubbles form.
4. Tell your child that you are going to pour some more water over their hands. Have your child rinse their hands, rubbing them together.
5. Use the towel to dry hands.
6. Notice how the water is dirty after washing. Compare the water in the bowl to the water in the pitcher if necessary.
7. Explain that we wash our hands to remove dirt and germs. You may also explain that dirt and germs can make us sick.

This lesson is useful to reinforce the importance of hand-washing even for children who have been washing their hands for a while on their own.

Independent Hand Washing

Teaching and encouraging independent hand washing is as much a lesson for children as for parents and caregivers. The lesson for parents is in ensuring that the necessary materials and tools are available for the child to perform this activity independently.

For handwashing success, parents and caregivers should make sure of the following:

- A stool should be provided so that children can reach the bathroom or kitchen sink easily. Older children may still need the stool to reach the faucet comfortably.
- Soap should be readily available. Bar soap or a pump variety are both fine. If using a pump, choose a soap dispenser that is not difficult to press down. Ensure that the soap is accessible for the child.
- The hand towel should be hung low so that the child can reach it easily

The process of teaching independent hand washing is simple and straight-forward. It can be incorporated into your daily routine and come up naturally. Demonstrate each step of hand-washing, and ask your child to try after observing.

1. If wearing long sleeves, show your child how to roll up their sleeves to avoid getting them wet while washing hands.
2. Turning on the water. Show your child how to turn on the water.
3. Wet hands. Show your child how to wet their hands carefully. Then, turn off the water.
4. Soap. Demonstrate how to rub soap from the bar or push down on the soap dispenser.
5. Suds. Demonstrate scrubbing your hands together until bubbles are formed, rubbing both the front and back of the hands. Remember to rub in between fingers and up to the wrists.
6. Turn on the water again and rinse off the hands until there is no soap left.
7. Dry hands on the towel.

One easy way to notice if hands have been washed properly is if the towel becomes dirty after drying. Continue to monitor your child as they master the skill of handwashing. When necessary, remind your child of the steps or invite them to wash their hands with you in order to watch the steps again.

Taking A Bath

Most young children enjoy bathing as it's a pleasant experience to play in the water. As your child approaches the age of 2, you can teach him or her to bathe more independently. However, do remember that for safety reasons, supervision while bathing is recommended to avoid slips and falls.

In order to help a child become more independent at bath time, some helpful items to have on hand are:

- A small bowl for pouring water
- A washcloth
- A rubber mat for the bottom of the tub

In addition, you'll need soap, shampoo, a towel or carpet to step on after the bath and a towel for drying the body. A bathrobe is also nice to have.

To reach independent bathing, use the usual bath routine you have with your child with some modifications. As your child grows, you can give him or her new responsibilities that are age appropriate. Below is a suggested order:

- Using a washcloth and soap to wash. Show your child how to rub the washcloth on the soap and then on his or her body. This is a great opportunity to name each part of the body as you wash.
- Shampooing hair. At first, you may want to put the shampoo in your child's hand. As he or she shows greater control and ability, your child can pour out the shampoo themselves. Show them how to scrub their head and hair, ensuring that all areas are reached.

- Children can use the small bowl to pour water over themselves in order to rinse. Show them how to get fresh water from the faucet and how to fill the bowl. Allow them to pour the water over their head and body.
- Once rinsed, the child should be helped out of the bathtub depending on the age and ability of your child. When you feel confident that he or she can do it on their own, allow them to do so.
- Once out, their towel should be in an easily accessible place such as low hook. Show your child how to dry off and wrap the towel around themselves.

For additional independence, you may consider using a bathrobe and a pair of slippers for your little one to use to walk from the bathroom to the bedroom. This is safer than walking using just a towel. Following the bath, continue with your normal dressing routine. Each time your child bathes, encourage them to complete more and more of the tasks on their own until they are able to complete the routine from beginning to end.

Taking a Shower

Similar to taking a bath, taking a shower involves the same basic steps. Make a point of encouraging your child to perform each of the steps on their own until he or she is able to shower independently. Supervision is recommended during this age range to avoid slips and falls.

Some children may feel an aversion to the shower and how the water falls on them, finding it an uncomfortable sensation. If available, a moveable shower attachment can sometimes help children become comfortable with the shower, as they have greater control over where the water falls. Other children enjoy the shower and have no trouble adjusting.

Another option for teaching this routine is a joint shower with parent and child, if both are comfortable with the idea. This saves time, water, and provides an opportunity to model proper bathing techniques.

Nudity in the home is ultimately up to the parents. If or when either parents or children become uncomfortable, it's best to avoid it. However, when nudity is seen as a normal part of life, sex therapist Dr. Dennis Sugrue says that this may actually be good for children. Researchers have found that children who grew up in homes where nudity was normal are more likely to grow up feeling comfortable with and accepting of their bodies and sexuality.

Washing the Face

In the morning and after meal times, it may be necessary for your child to wash their face. This can easily be taught so that your child can perform this task whenever he or she feels it's necessary.

The materials to wash the face should be made available so that your child can reach them whenever he or she wishes. Find a space in the bathroom to keep these items:

- Soap (mild soap that will not irritate the skin)
- A washcloth
- A towel
- A mirror, easy for the child to see

The following steps can be used to teach your child how to wash their face:

1. Show your child the special place where the materials are kept. Place the necessary items within reach on a countertop.

2. Roll up sleeves. If your child is wearing a long-sleeved shirt, show them how to push the sleeves back.
3. Turn on the water. Show your child how to adjust the water temperature.
4. Wet the face. Show your child how to use their hands to get the face wet.
5. Then, show them how to get the washcloth wet. Turn off the faucet.
6. Apply soap to the washcloth. Scrub the washcloth until it becomes sudsy.
7. Show your child how to gently scrub the cheeks, forehead and nose, without getting soap in the eyes.
8. Show your child how to set the cloth aside on the counter. Turn the water on again and rinse the face using the hands.
9. Use the towel to dry the face.
10. Rinse off the washcloth with the running water. Then turn off the water and squeeze out the washcloth. The washcloth can be hung up again to use later.

This lesson can be made exciting by announcing to your child that you think they are ready to wash their face all by themselves. Invite your child to the space you plan to use for washing the face, typically the bathroom, and show them where the materials will be kept. Most young children are excited about being given added responsibility in their lives. It encourages their sense of independence.

Combing Hair

For this lesson, explain to your child that you are going to show them how to comb their own hair. Prepare a space where you are going to keep the necessary materials so that your child can access them. A low drawer in the bathroom is one option.

Materials necessary:
- Comb
- Brush
- Mirror the child can easily see

Show your child where the materials are kept. Place all items on the counter. If necessary, set up a small mirror on the counter in the bathroom or use a stool to see a larger mirror. Then, after demonstrating, invite your child to comb his or her hair, beginning at the top of the head and pulling down to the sides. Invite your child to look in the mirror to observe their appearance. When finished, invite your child to put the materials back in their spot.

Remind your child that throughout the day, they can check their appearance in the mirror and comb their hair if necessary.

Children with longer hair can be shown how to use simple clips and ponytail holders as they become old enough to handle them.

Blowing the Nose

This lesson can often be taught informally, when it comes up in everyday life. By being prepared as a caregiver, you can give this lesson when you feel your child is ready. Blowing the nose is a lesson that's most effective when your child really needs to, as this will make the purpose of the lesson clear to your child. In order to complete this lesson, you'll need:

- Kleenex or a handkerchief
- Wastebasket (if using Kleenex)
- Mirror

The steps that for this lesson are:

1. Notice that your child has a runny nose. Comment on this. For example, "It looks like you have a runny nose."

2. Tell your child "I'm going to show you how to blow your nose."
3. Go to, or get the mirror. Observe the runny nose.
4. Get out the Kleenex or handkerchief. Show your child how to fold it and demonstrate blowing your nose gently.
5. Give a Kleenex or handkerchief to your child and ask them to try.
6. Wipe the nose completely.
7. Look in the mirror to ensure that the face is clean.
8. If using Kleenex, throw it away in the wastebasket and ask your child to do the same.

As a follow up, explain to your child that he or she should wash their hands after blowing the nose. Also, show your child where they can find Kleenex or a handkerchief so that they may freely blow their nose whenever necessary.

Sneezing/Coughing into Elbow

Sneezing and coughing can spread germs to others. The elbow is the best option for covering up a sneeze or cough, as it's unlikely that the inner elbow will come into contact with other people or objects.

Most children don't attempt to cover a sneeze or cough. However, with gentle reminders and practice sessions, your child can make covering up with their elbow a habit. First, demonstrate to your child how you would do it. Encourage your child to try, pretending to cough or sneeze. Then, each time your child coughs or sneezes, remind them to use their elbow until it becomes habit.

Applying Lotion

This lesson can be helpful in getting your child comfortable with applying cream to the body, and is good preparation for applying sunscreen. It's also useful for healing dry skin that children may have on their hands, arms or on other areas of the body.

Materials needed:
- Body lotion of your choice, preferably in a small bottle
- A mirror

Show your child how to get an appropriate amount of lotion out and rub it in on the area of the body that is dry. Use the mirror to check if the lotion has been rubbed in completely. No white streaks should be visible.

Some children enjoy putting lotion on others and it can be a great way to practice using lotion correctly.

Clipping Nails

Appropriate for children approaching the age of 6, this activity must be taught with care. Use your best judgement to determine if your child will be able to clip their own nails safely. Be sure to use guided practice in which you assist by watching your child the first few times they complete this activity on their own.

The materials needed are:
- A tray
- Nail clippers
- Wastebasket

To begin, help your child notice when their nails are getting too long. It's useful if you trim your nails alongside your child. So, if possible, ensure that both you and your child need to trim your nails. The following are some helpful steps to follow:

1. Show your child your nails and say something along the lines of "My nails are getting too long. I need to clip them. Let's check yours." After determining that both of you need to clip your nails, invite your child to do it together.
2. Show your child where to get the necessary supplies, ensuring that they are accessible to your child.
3. Use a well-lit space, preferably a table.
4. Show your child how to open the nail clippers. Ask them to try.
5. Demonstrate placing your hands over the tray and begin clipping one hand's nails. It's good to go in order, from thumb to pinky.
6. Assist your child as they begin to clip their nails.
7. When finished, show your child how to tilt the tray carefully and dump the nail clippings into the wastebasket.
8. Put the items used away.

When finished, observe your nails again and notice that they are not too long anymore. Remind your child to wash their hands after completing the activity.

"We must help them to learn how to walk without assistance, to run, to go up and down the stairs, to pick up fallen objects, to dress and undress, to wash themselves, to express their needs, and to attempt to satisfy their desires through their own efforts. All this is part of an education for independence."
- DR. MARIA MONTESSORI

CHAPTER FOUR

Dressing

Getting undressed is usually learned much more quickly and easily than dressing. What parent hasn't chased after a nude little one through the house after said little one learned how to pull of her socks and pants? Dressing involves quite a number of skills. Fine motor skills, coordination and a solid understanding of how clothing works are all requirements for dressing successfully.

The Montessori curriculum encourages children to isolate the skills necessary for dressing to help children improve their concentration, motor skills and coordination. With these skills in place, children then have an easier time dressing.

Montessori preschool classrooms include several dressing activities and rituals. Some of the most well-known are the dressing frames (teaching everything from zippers to buttons and buckles) and the shoe-changing ritual. Before entering the classroom, children must change from outdoor shoes to indoor shoes. Before going outdoors, they must also change from indoor shoes to outdoor shoes. This ritual is meant to increase independence and also helps keep the classroom floor clean, which is of particular importance because children often work on the floor.

This emphasis on dressing is, as Montessori said, part of the "education for independence". Montessori believed that through their independence, children became ever more able in their learning. Through independence, children are able to pursue their own interests, work hard based out of their own motivation, and discover the world around them.

The following lessons have been chosen to include in this guide. Each lesson includes guidelines, materials and suggestions for how to present the lesson.

- Dressing Frames:
    - Zipping/unzipping
- Putting clothes in the laundry basket
- Putting on shoes and rain boots
- Putting on a jacket
- Putting on pants
- Putting on a hat
- Putting on socks
- Putting on a belt
- Folding clothes
- Hanging up clothes
- Choosing appropriate clothing
- Making the bed
- Sewing a button
- How to use an umbrella

Many of these activities can be taught as a part of your daily routine. Other activities can be taught in a special way and made available for your child to continue practicing as he or she chooses. As with all Montessori activities, some preparation on your part to ensure that your child has access to the items will be necessary.

As you present these lessons to your child, remember to be patient and observe your child. If your child doesn't seem very interested or the activity seems too difficult, you can try again another time. Avoid pushing or forcing your child to complete an activity as this will create resistance. With time, it's likely that your child will accept your invitation to learn a skill and quickly acquire it once he or she decides to practice it.

Dressing Frames

Dressing frames can easily be made or purchased so that your child can practice some of the basic skills used in getting dressed. Some of the most important ones to include are: zipping/unzipping, buttoning/unbuttoning and snapping/unsnapping. However, you may include other frames including buckles, Velcro, and tying bows as needed, depending on the interests of your child. A shoe-tying dressing frame is often popular among older children reaching the age of 5 or 6.

Each dressing frame consists of a wooden frame with two pieces of fabric stretched across it, simulating the front of a jacket or shirt. The fabric can be joined using zippers, buttons, snaps or another fastening mechanism.

Each frame should be presented separately. Introduce them one at a time, giving your child a day or two in between presentations. You can leave the frames out in your child's room in a basket so that they can practice as they please.

Here are some helpful steps for presenting a frame: (Please note the instructions are written for right-handed children. Try to demonstrate using the opposite hand if your child is left-handed.)

Zipping/Unzipping

1. Invite your child to try something new with you.

2. Show your child the dressing frame. Place it on a table or on a carpet on the floor you've set out to work on.
3. Use your left hand to steady the cloth on the left-hand side of the zipper, gently holding the cloth at the top of the frame.
4. Grab the zipper piece with your right hand and gently pull it down all the way to the bottom until the zipper is released.
5. Bring your left hand to the bottom of the frame, grabbing the bottom, left-hand side to steady the bottom of the zipper. Use your right hand to insert the slider piece onto the zipper chain.
6. Once the slider has been successfully inserted, pinch the bottom of the zipper with your left hand and gently pull up on the slider with your right hand, until the zipper has been zipped again.
7. Ask your child if they'd like to try.
8. Repeat the demonstration as necessary.

A similar approach can be used for all of the dressing frames. Ensure that you make the movements slowly and deliberately so that your child can watch.

Instead of correcting your child when making a mistake, allow them to continue working. If your child shows frustration, ask if they would like your help. By refraining from interfering, you allow your child to actually learn more as they've spent more time manipulating the material. If your child accepts your help, demonstrate the action again, and allow your child to try to repeat. Encourage your child to continue practicing by inviting them to use the material until they've mastered the activity.

Putting Clothes in the Laundry Basket

Even children at age 2 or even younger can participate in this activity. Place a laundry basket in a convenient location in your child's room, or in another location that's easily accessible for your child. Whenever your child undresses, ask them to place the clothes in the laundry basket.

When there are obvious stains or the clothes smell bad, you can use this as an opportunity to explain why the clothes need to go in the laundry basket. Invite your child to observe the dirt on the clothes or smell them. Ask your child to always put their dirty clothes in the laundry basket.

Providing accessible hooks for sweaters, pajamas or other clothing items that can be reused is an easy way to give your child an option to hang up clothes that don't belong in the hamper. Encourage your child to differentiate between clean and dirty clothing, putting dirty clothes in the laundry basket.

Putting on Shoes and Rain Boots

Shoes and rain boots can be a challenge for young children. The first point parents need to consider when planning this lesson is the type of shoes provided for their children. For children ages 2-4, shoes with simple fasteners like Velcro are best. As they grow in their ability by using the dressing frames and other tools, buckle and lace shoes may be purchased. The child should be able to manipulate the shoe successfully in order to put them on and take them off independently.

Similarly, rain boots with handles on the sides or a pull on the back of the boot can often be purchased to make them easier for children to handle.

Additionally, parents must create a space for children to keep their shoes. A shoe rack or wooden crate near the entrance of your home or in your child's room will do. Remember to provide a stool so that your child may sit to put on and take off their shoes comfortably.

Show your child basic techniques such as holding the tongue of the shoe back or holding on to the heel of the shoe with their fingers. Some parents find it helpful to cut a sticker (of a smiley face or animal for example) in half, and place half in each shoe. This way, when put side by side, children can see that they are putting the correct shoe on (right and left) because the sticker makes a picture.

Remind your child where to keep their shoes. When they put them away properly, you can reinforce this with a comment that shows the benefit of their actions. For example: "Thanks for putting your shoes away. Now I won't trip over them." Or "Thanks for putting your shoes away. Now you'll know where to find them."

Lastly, you need to choose to give your child the space to practice this activity. So often we parents are in a hurry to get things done and get out the door. Start your process a few minutes earlier and encourage your young child to try putting their shoes on by themselves. Giving space for this activity is sometimes tough. We'd love to swoop in and get those shoes on or off quickly. By refraining unless your child asks for help, your child will slowly improve upon their skills and eventually master this task.

Putting on a Jacket

This simple task can be difficult for the youngest of children. With practice the opportunity to do it on their own, children can master this skill at a young age. In your routine, remember to encourage your child to try putting on their jacket on their own. You can help by providing jackets with simple closures such as large buttons or a zipper. Ensure that your child has easy access to his or her jacket, and that they know where it belongs. Low hooks close to your door are a convenient option.

Putting on Pants

To help children succeed in putting on pants independently, it's best to start with easy to handle items such as pants with an elastic waistband. Show your child any features such as pockets on the pants in order to help them differentiate the front from the back.

A dressing stool may be provided so that it's easier to practice putting pants on. A helpful order for the lesson might be:

1. Invite your child to try something new.
2. Ensure your child is wearing only underwear and a top. Invite your child to sit on the stool.
3. Show your child the pants and discuss any features. Help your child hold the pants, front side up.
4. Encourage your child to hold the pants open, placing thumbs on the inside of the pants and the other fingers outside.
5. Notice the two holes.
6. Encourage your child to place one leg in one hole, and the other leg in the other hole.
7. Ask your child to stand up and pull the pants up.
8. Explain to your child that from now on, they may put their pants on by themselves.

Putting on a Hat

This activity is fairly easy to master. Keep your child's hats in an easy to access place such as a low drawer or set of hooks in their bedroom. When going out in the sun or cold, encourage your child to find a hat and put it on. If necessary, demonstrate how to put a hat on.

Putting on Socks

Socks can be deceptively tricky. It seems like a simple task, but in addition to pulling them on, children must identify the heel and top side. Additionally, socks often fit quite snugly, which means it can be tough for little fingers to pull hard enough on the socks to get them on.

Similar to the lesson on putting on pants, you can show your child each step of putting on socks. This one is easy to do alongside your child, showing how you find the top of the sock, carefully hold the sock open and pull it over your foot.

Putting on a Belt

Before presenting this lesson, it's helpful if your child has experience using buckles either on a dressing frame or with shoes. You may also consider practicing with the belt by wrapping it around a pillow. This way, your child can grow accustomed to manipulating the buckle before performing this task while wearing the belt.

Additionally, before showing your child how to thread the belt through belt loops, it's helpful if your child has experience stringing beads or similar. This way, the concept of threading is not completely new.

Finally, it's often easier for children to thread the belt through the pants before putting them on until they become more proficient at the skill.

Folding Clothes

This important skill helps children take care of their clothing and contribute to household chores. It's easiest to start with simple clothing such as washcloths and handkerchiefs that can simply be folded in squares. Then, children can move on to fold more difficult items such as pants, t-shirts, sweaters and socks.

Many Montessori programs use photos in addition to demonstrations for teaching clothes folding. That way, after a demonstration, a child can use the photos of the different stages of clothes folding to check their work. For example, for folding pants, you might take 3 photos:

1. Photo 1: The pants laid out smooth on a table.
2. Photo 2: The pants folded in half (one pant leg over the other)
3. Photo 3: The pants folded in half once more, from hem to waist.

These can be placed on laminated cards with numbers (1, 2, 3) so the child can also practice putting them in order. When folding pants, the child can simply set up the cards and follow the steps using real pants.

Folding clothes is a great activity to do together, parent and child. For the first few times your child helps you fold clothes, avoid distractions by taking only 2 handkerchiefs to a table, one for you and one for your child. If you dump out a full laundry basket, your child may become interested in the rest of the clothes, rather than the lesson. At the table, demonstrate each fold and ask your child to repeat after you.

Allow your child to practice with handkerchiefs as many times as he or she wishes.

Another strategy that can be helpful in teaching young children to fold clothes is to sew along the lines where your child needs to fold. Use a handkerchief, washcloth or cloth napkin. This helps your child identify how to fold in half, and in half again. Use a color of thread that contrasts with the color of the handkerchief or similar item.

Hanging Up Clothes

Some clothing items such as coats, jackets, dresses, sweaters and dress shirts are best kept hanging up. Create a space for your child to hang up clothes. You can do this easily by modifying a closet, placing a lower clothing rod, or you can fashion one that is stand-free. It's also best to use child-sized hangers, as small clothing doesn't fit well on larger hangers.

Once you have this space set up for your child, take the time to introduce them to the idea. Here are some helpful steps:

1. Invite your child to try something new.
2. Present them with one item of clothing to be hung on a hanger. Lay it out on the bed or a table.
3. Show them the hanger.
4. Carefully insert the hanger, so that the clothing item hangs from it.
5. Pick up the hanger off the bed, and hang it on the rod.
6. Explain to your child that clothing doesn't get as wrinkly this way.
7. Invite your child to try.

Choosing Appropriate Clothing

For this activity, your child will need to have an awareness of the weather and the different activities that they engage in. You can increase this awareness by noticing the weather when you go outside together. You can also talk about your own clothing choices. For example, you can say "I'm going to bake today, and that's messy. So I'm going to wear some old jeans and an apron." This building of awareness can be part of your daily routine together.

Encourage your child to start making decisions about what clothing to wear in the mornings or after a bath. Help your child think through it. For example, if your child bathes in the evening and will go to sleep soon, you can say "I think you can help me pick out the right clothes. It's dark outside and will soon be time to go to sleep. What do we wear for sleeping?" Help your child pick out pajamas.

Through this process of asking and encouraging your child to pick out clothing, they will slowly build their confidence until they can easily pick out clothes for any occasion on their own.

Making the Bed

As your child grows you'll notice that they become ever more skilled at controlling their movements. When you think your child is ready, invite him or her to help you make the bed. This activity is easiest for children when they can walk around at least 3 sides of the bed, usually the head of the bed is against a wall. Show your child how to gently pull the sheets and blankets up to the top of the bed, first on one side and then on the other.

You can continue to teach your child new skills in bed making as they grow. For instance, how to change a pillow cover or how to place

Sewing a Button

Sewing a button, and any sewing is quite exciting and helpful for young children. It helps develop their concentration and improves fine motor skills. Before diving in with replacing a button, try a few lead up activities first.

For instance, your child should have practice tying a knot in order to sew successfully. Pre-sewing activities such as inserting yarn through cardboard sewing boards is also a great lead-in activity. Once your child has tried a few of these, then you can move on to button-related projects.

One of my favorites is making a button bracelet. The necessary materials to teach this lesson include:

- Easy to handle fabric such as felt or fleece
- Large needle
- Yarn or embroidery thread
- Scissors
- Large button

Cut the fabric into a long rectangle, long enough to wrap comfortably around your child's wrist. Then cut a sliver on one end that will be the button hole. Place all of the materials on a tray and invite your child to the lesson.

1. Explain to your child that today you're going to sew a button.
2. Ask your child to cut a piece of thread. You can help them measure a piece that's about as long as your forearm.
3. Then show them the needle. Show them the pointy end and the eye. Remind them to be careful. Then, have them thread the needle with the thread.

4. Tie a knot at the end of the thread.
5. Show your child the button, and have them place it on the end of the fabric, the end opposite of the buttonhole.
6. Ask them to use the needle to poke a hole in the fabric, draw it through and draw it through the button. You may choose to demonstrate on your own bracelet.
7. Show your child how to sew the button on, repeating the stitches until the button is secured.
8. Then, show your child how to tie another knot to close off the stitching.
9. Cut off any extra thread.
10. Show your child how to put the "button bracelet" on.

If your child enjoys this activity, you may encourage them to make several button bracelets for friends or family members. Then, you may show your child how to replace a button on a piece of clothing or work on other sewing projects together.

How to Use an Umbrella

Children often love going out in the rain. They enjoy the novelty of rain boots and an umbrella. With a child-sized umbrella, young children can easily learn to open, carry and close the umbrella. Much like the approach suggested in other lessons, parents can show step by step how to use the umbrella. To begin it can often be easier to teach indoors. Learning to open and close the umbrella safely without pinching fingers should be the first goal.

In addition to the skills needed for using an umbrella, parents should also encourage the proper etiquette and awareness. For example, take care not to spin the umbrella, as it may spray water on others. Another helpful guideline might be to notice surroundings when opening and closing the umbrella to avoid hitting other people or objects. Finally, children need to learn the proper behavior for handling a wet umbrella. Is the wet umbrella left on the porch open to dry? Or should it be closed and placed in a container that will hold the dripping water? The answers to these questions may be different for each family, but by teaching expectations ahead of time, parents can avoid accidents or undesired behavior.

"Any child who is self-sufficient, who can tie his shoes, dress or undress himself, reflects in his joy and sense of achievement the image of human dignity, which is derived from a sense of independence."
- DR. MARIA MONTESSORI

CHAPTER FIVE

Food

Food is an integral part of daily life and necessary for nutrition. In social settings, food also plays an important role. Children must learn not only the physical and practical aspects of eating, but also the etiquette and manners associated with meal and snack times.

For children from ages 2-6, children gradually learn eating and food related skills, from chewing carefully to handling utensils and serving. In addition, children become much more expressive at mealtime and begin to notice social behaviors surrounding food.

The lessons included in this chapter are intended to help you address some of the skills children should develop surrounding food in the age span from 2-6:

- Chewing and swallowing food
- Drinking from a cup
- Using utensils (spoon, fork, knife)
- Using a napkin at mealtime
- Pouring a drink
- Serving a snack

Chewing and Swallowing Food

By the age of 2, children are already eating just about anything, although some children may still have trouble with very hard crunchy foods such as raw carrots or nuts. The concern about chewing and swallowing at this age is largely related to manners and ensuring that appropriate sized bites are being taken.

Some young children take very large bites, or stuff too much food in their mouth at once. Or, sometimes chewing with the mouth open becomes a habit.

These issues can be discussed at mealtime and snack-time. The key to success in this area is how the topic is discussed. Rather than scolding, say to your child, "I wonder if you can take small bites so that the food fits nicely in your mouth." This sort of approach will likely achieve greater cooperation.

Drinking from a Cup

Many families use sippy cups because they are convenient. However, these cups deny children the experiences of real life. Montessori encouraged children to be given real objects, including fragile ones. When a cup is turned over, the liquid spills. If a glass is dropped, it breaks. These cause and effect lessons must be experienced by young children. Not only does it teach them about how the world works, but it helps them advance on their journey to learn to control their movements.

Allow your child to learn these skills and have these experiences by giving them real cups and glasses. Even a two-year-old can learn to be careful enough to use a cup or glass. Keep the use of sippy cups limited to car trips. For other outings, you can take a bottle with a cup into which to pour the drink.

Using Utensils

You can help your child become more proficient at using utensils through modeling and teaching techniques.

The first utensil used by children is often the spoon. Food can be cut up into bite sized pieces so that the spoon can be used to scoop them up. If you still spoon feed your child, consider transferring the responsibility to your child slowly. Give your child a spoon and continue to spoon feed your child. After a few meals in this fashion, stop spoon feeding your child and allow them to do it on their own.

Once your child has mastered the spoon, present them with the fork. Pieces of chicken, cooked vegetables or even cheese are great for practicing. First, demonstrate how to use the fork yourself and then allow your child to try.

Finally, your child may be introduced to the knife. Young children usually love using a butter knife and learning to cut. Use slices of watermelon, cheese and bananas to start. This is a great way for your child to learn to slice carefully and enjoy a healthy snack.

Using a Napkin at Mealtime

Wiping the face with a hand or a sleeve seems to be almost instinctual. Children can very quickly develop this habit. However, with gentle reminders and the provision of a napkin, children can learn to use this instead. If possible, use cloth napkins as these are more durable.

Ensure that napkins are kept in a low place where your child can access them. This way, whenever your child has a snack and needs to wipe his or her face, they can easily grab one.

Pouring a Drink

Pouring is a great activity to improve independence and develop fine motor control. Present this lesson when you believe your child is ready and afterwards, make the necessary materials available at snack and meal time so that your child can practice.

Necessary items:

- Small glass or ceramic pitcher about ¾ full of water
- Small (juice sized) glasses
- A cloth for wiping up spills

Place the items out on a child-sized table and invite your child to try something new:

1. Explain to your child that today you are going to show them how to pour a glass of water.
2. Take the pitcher with your dominant hand on the handle. Use your non-dominant hand to support the front of the pitcher.
3. Tip the pitcher to pour water into one of the glasses.
4. Place the pitcher back on the table carefully.
5. Invite your child to try.
6. If any spills occur, show your child how to wipe it up with the cloth.

Serving a Snack

In Montessori preschool classrooms, children regularly serve their own snacks. Healthy options are provided for children to choose from. The entire process, from preparation to eating and clean-up is carried out by the students. This can also work within your home.

Some options for healthy snacks that children can easily prepare on their own are:

- Crackers with cream cheese
- Peanut butter and jelly sandwiches
- Clementines or mandarins
- Bananas
- Raisins
- Water

These can be kept in a space where your child can easily access them, such as a low cupboard and a low shelf in the refrigerator. Also make plates, glasses, butter knives, napkins, toothpicks and cleaning cloths available to your child so that they can carry out the preparation and clean up independently. Ideally, a child sized table and chair and child sized broom and dustpan are also made available to your child.

Once the necessary materials are ready, you can invite your child to the lesson.

1. First, show your child where the snack items are kept.
2. Choose a snack together and get the necessary items out.
3. Show your child how to prepare the snack. Bananas can be cut into slices and toothpicks placed in each slice for added interest.
4. Have your child pour water to drink.
5. Enjoy the snack together.
6. Then, notice if any crumbs have been dropped on the table or the floor.
7. Put all snack items away together.
8. Show your child how to clean up with the cloth and broom and dustpan.

9. Explain to your child that whenever he or she feels hungry and would like a snack, that they may now prepare it and clean up on their own.

"... in order for children to develop independence in any realm, or develop any other human potential for that matter, they must be given the freedom to act..."
- DR. MARIA MONTESSORI

Chapter Six

Safety

In addition to caring for their own basic needs in dressing, hygiene and eating, self-care for young children also includes awareness of safety practices and concerns. Learning to be aware of their surroundings and knowing how to respond to a wide variety of situations greatly increases safety and self-sufficiency. By taking a proactive approach, parents and caregivers can teach valuable lessons that will prepare their children to act with confidence both within and outside the home.

When dealing with safety topics, try to use a matter of fact tone and avoid scaring your child with unnecessary details. For children between the ages of 2 and 6, there is a wide range of understanding and ability to discuss the abstract. Abstract concepts are still quite difficult to understand for younger children. Lessons that require abstract thinking should be saved for older children who are between the ages of 4 and 6. Use your judgement when choosing lessons appropriate for your child. Give simple, basic explanations to questions that come up.

The topics that will be addressed include:
- Applying Sunscreen
- Applying Bug Repellent
- Knowing Parent's Names

- Learning Last Names
- Learning the Address
- Learning Phone Numbers
- Awareness of Surroundings
- Reading Basic Signs
- Learning to Call 911
- Basic First Aid
- Fire Safety
- Strangers
- Traffic Lights
- Looking for Helpers
- Identifying First Responders
- What to Do in a Tornado

Applying Sunscreen

Sunscreen should be used any time your child will experience prolonged exposure to the sun. Help your child learn how to apply sunscreen independently by keeping sunscreen in a small bottle in a place where your child can easily get to it. Then, discuss the circumstances under which your child should apply sunscreen.

For the first time that your child applies sunscreen, provide a mirror. You may also wish to provide a drawing or picture highlighting the parts of the body where you want your child to apply sunscreen. Depending on the clothes your child is wearing, have them apply sunscreen to the face, neck, and arms.

Show your child how to squeeze out a small amount of sunscreen and apply it to the face, rubbing it in until no white streaks are left. Do the same for the other areas of the body, checking in the mirror to ensure the cream has been rubbed in fully.

Encourage your child to apply sunscreen every time they play or participate in an outside activity in the sun.

Applying Bug Repellent

Whether you use traditional or a natural bug repellent, your child can learn when and how to use it properly. Natural bug repellents are generally safer, and more recommendable for children to use on their own. When using traditional bug repellents, although the child may be able to apply it, this should always be done under supervision.

Natural bug repellants can be kept in a spray bottle or used as a cream. When mosquitos and other biting insects are plentiful, explain to your child that bug repellent can help them avoid being bitten. Invite your child to apply the bug repellent to all exposed areas of their body, except for the face, and to wash their hands afterwards.

Traditional repellents require additional care as some of the ingredients can be dangerous. Ensure that your child doesn't apply the repellent near the eyes or mouth and that hands are washed thoroughly afterwards.

Knowing Parent's Names

In the unfortunate event that your child should get lost, it's important that he or she know the names of caregivers and parents. While this seems obvious, many children only know their parents as "Mommy" and "Daddy" or similar.

Without needing to describe a scary situation, you can take the time to teach your children their parent's and caregiver's names. In addition to simply asking and repeating, you may also want to create a small booklet or nomenclature cards of important family members.

Nomenclature or 3-part cards are an integral part of Montessori preschool classrooms. To make them, print off two copies of each picture to be used (6-8 family members is a great number to start with). Paste the pictures onto cardstock and cut them out, so that there is one picture on each card. On one set of pictures, type or write the name of the person below their picture. On the second set, don't provide any labels. On small strips of paper, type or write the names of the family members.

To use the cards, show your child the set with names attached to your child. Name each person and set them out in a vertical row on the table. Then, show your child a picture of a family member from the other set. Show your child how you find the match and place the photo to the right of the match. Then, ask your child to match the rest of the unlabeled photos to the labeled photos. Then, do the same with the labels. The labels can be reserved for when your child grows older and can begin to distinguish between letters. However, 3 and 4-year-olds can often match words even if they are not yet able to read.

Learning Last Names

If your child doesn't know their last name, take the time to teach it. Often by simply repeating, children can learn their full name. Older children who are interested may enjoy tracing their full name using crayons or colored pencils.

This information is also important in the event that your child should get lost.

Learning the Address

Knowing the home address can help greatly in many safety situations, from reporting an emergency to finding the home of a lost child. By the age of 5 or 6, most children can memorize quite a bit of information, including an address.

As with the other lessons, it need not be presented as a safety concern, but knowing this personal detail would certainly be helpful in an emergency situation.

An easy way to explain addresses is to tell your child that every house has a special number so that other people can easily find it. A similar explanation also works for street and city names.

Children may enjoy tracing over or writing their address. As an extension, you could have your child send letters to family members or friends. This requires writing the return address, giving an opportunity for your child to practice the information.

Learning Phone Numbers

It's best if children can memorize the phone number most often used by their parents, whether it be a home phone number or cell phone. Once one number has been memorized, another one can be added.

To encourage learning and memorizing phone numbers, you may consider making a small phone book together where your child can keep phone numbers of family members and friends. Once you've made it, explain to your child that they may wish to call someone when the phone book is not available. Discuss together which number would be the most important to learn, and practice memorizing it together.

Awareness of Surroundings

Through a variety of activities, children can learn to notice more about their surroundings. Although children are naturally very observant and curious, while playing or concentrating on an activity, they can become blind to what's going on around them. A heightened awareness of surroundings can help increase the safety of your child in a number of ways. For example, the risk of falling can be reduced and they are less likely to bump into others.

You can encourage a greater awareness in your child through routine conversations and open-ended questions. For example, if you visit a new park, you might notice any muddy spots together. You might also look at where the swings are and talk together about what might happen if they walk in front of the space where others are swinging. By regularly making observations of new places together, your child can grow in their awareness skills.

Reading Basic Signs

There are many signs that use images or graphics to communicate. Colors, stick people and arrows are often used. By teaching your child some of these basic signs, you can ensure their safety. Some good signs to start with are: stop sign, dangerous substance sign, women's and men's bathroom signs, hot sign, caution sign, and slippery sign. You can make nomenclature cards or a small book of these signs to practice them.

Learning to Call 911

Prevention and preparedness is important in every household. Even a child as young as 4 can help by calling 911 should a parent or caregiver be unable to do so. This lesson needs to communicate the importance of performing this action while also stressing that 911 is only for emergencies when an adult is unable to help.

For young children, understanding an emergency can be difficult. Give some examples for emergencies such as: a big fire in the house, or mommy or daddy won't wake up, or mommy or daddy is bleeding and won't talk to you.

So that your child is prepared to perform this action, have your child practice making other phone calls to family members or friends. You can post 911 on the refrigerator and explain to your child that this is the emergency number and that when this number is called, the police, ambulance or firefighters will come. If you've already made a phone book with your child, include 911 in the book.

Basic First Aid

Some basic knowledge in first aid can help assuage children's fears when minor scrapes, cuts and bruises occur. Handling these situations on their own increases their independence and self-confidence.

Make Band-aids, antibacterial cream and ice packs available to your child. If your freezer is inaccessible for children, tell your child to ask for an ice pack when necessary. Teach your child the basic procedure for handling a scrape or cut. For example:

1. Wash the wound.
2. Dry the area around the cut or scrape completely.
3. Apply antibacterial cream.
4. Place a Band-aid over the wound.

For a bruise on the head that creates a goose-egg, explain to your child that an ice-pack can help the bump go away. After going through the procedure with your child together several times, tell your child that the next time they get a cut, scrape or bruise that you think they're ready to handle it on their own.

Fire Safety

Every family should have a basic fire plan. Part of the plan involves explaining to children what to do in case of a fire. There is a great deal that can be taught relating to fire safety. Only the basics will be covered here. For further information about how to make a family fire plan, contact your local fire department.

Stop, drop and roll

For this lesson, your child should be able to understand abstract concepts and pretend play. Explain to your child that sometimes fire does unexpected things. Tell them that if their clothing or hair ever catches on fire, they should follow this procedure: stop, drop and roll. Demonstrate each step and ask your child to copy. Then, you might consider a role-playing game, where the parent and child notice that one of them has caught on fire, and then practice the appropriate response.

Recognizing a smoke alarm

Your child should be familiar with smoke alarms, their purpose and what they sound like. You may choose to take advantage of the time when you perform routine maintenance to your smoke alarms to have your child walk with you throughout the house. Notice the smoke alarms together, explain their purpose and test them to ensure the batteries work. Tell your child that if they hear the alarm, they should go outside. Decide exactly where you want your child to go. For example, pick a tree or other landmark on your property such as the mailbox. That way, you will know exactly where to find your children.

Strangers and Other Dangers

Some children are friendly and talkative while others are more reserved. In either case, for your child's safety, a discussion about strangers and routine reminders about the topic are helpful. Additionally, children should also know that they can tell you about any scary or uncomfortable situations they encounter. Sexual abuse perpetrators are often known to the victim. Clear communication about what's ok behavior and what's not ok can help your child know what to do.

Some books are also helpful in discussing this topic. For example:
- Your Body Belongs to You by Cornelia Spelman
- The Berenstain Bears Learn About Strangers by Stan & Jan Berenstain
- I Said No! by Kimberly and Zack King

You may also want to provide your child with some rules or guidelines such as:
- A parent must always know where you are.
- Only accept food or candy from friends and family.
- If you ever feel uncomfortable with anyone, tell your parents or someone else you trust.

By implementing these rules or guidelines, you can help your child avoid potentially dangerous situations. Try to keep these conversations basic. Don't go into great detail about all of the bad things that can happen. Simply state that you want them to always be safe.

When discussing strangers, explain that not all strangers are bad, but that it's not good to trust people who aren't known well by the family.

With regards to sexual abuse, explain that some people may want to touch their private parts, or for them to touch theirs and this is not ok. Give your child clear actions such as screaming, saying "no" and telling you about it. Simple explanations should help your child understand without creating excessive fear.

Traffic Lights and Pedestrian Indicators

Flashing, bright lights are sure to draw the attention of children. With a basic understanding of how traffic lights and pedestrian indicators work, children can be safer while walking around town.

Pedestrian indicators are easy to explain and follow. You can easily teach your child how the indicators work while walking around town. Point out the different colors used in pedestrian signs and explain what they mean. Then, when crossing at the next corner, ask your child to let you know when it's ok to cross and how they know.

Traffic lights are also simple to explain. After observing them when driving or walking, you can enjoy some follow up activities. For instance, your child can color in a traffic light. Or, you can make 3 different circles and paste them to popsicle sticks. Hold each circle up and have your child respond as if they were a car (stopping on red, walking slowly on yellow and walking normally on green).

Identifying First Responders and Helpers

When children know who to get help from, it's more likely that they can find their way out of dangerous situations. For example, a child who gets lost, but can find a police officer, a crossing guard or other community member to help, will be able to make their way home more quickly.

One way to approach this lesson is by teaching professions and community members. These can be taught using nomenclature cards and pointing them out around town. Especially important to include here are police officers, firefighters, lifeguards and paramedics. Children should be able to identify each of these helpers and explain their job.

What to Do in a Tornado

If you live in an area where tornadoes occur, it's best to do some basic education about this natural disaster and how to stay safe. Some children may even experience tornado drills at school, so taking the time to talk about it at home can help alleviate anxiety surrounding the topic.

Start by showing your child videos or pictures of a tornado. Tell your child that tornadoes are a result of extreme weather and that it's very fast moving wind. Explain that although it's not likely that a tornado will occur close to your home, it's best to be prepared.

Then, go over your family's plans for dealing with a tornado. If you have a basement, this is the safest place to seek refuge during a tornado. Otherwise, agree on another location and show your child how to cover the back of his or her head to protect it.

"The greatest sign of success for a teacher is to be able to say, "The children are now working as if I did not exist."
- DR. MARIA MONTESSORI

CHAPTER SEVEN

Manners

From a young age, children copy and mimic adults. They notice our every move and word. This is also true when it comes to manners. While most of the time children strive to please their parents, and show quite pleasant temperaments, children between the ages of 2 and 6 are still mastering their abilities to reason and judge. Experts and researchers agree that the tantrums, that so famously give year 2 its nickname "the terrible twos", are a normal part of childhood.

In addition to the brain development that increases a child's ability to reason and judge between the years 2 and 6, children also must acquire the vocabulary and ability to communicate. This can be a frustrating process, sometimes ending in tears.

However, this doesn't mean that manners can't be taught and learned during this time. Children can be introduced to many lessons about manners that will help them develop excellent habits in this area for life. People skills and the ability to empathize with others, among other skills, will determine the success of your child's future relationships, personal and professional.

Teaching manners, people skills and healthy ways of expressing emotions are the focus of the lessons included in this book. In the Montessori classroom, these are also referred to as "Grace and Courtesy" lessons. They are:

- Calming Down
- Being Thankful
- Saying "please"
- Saying "sorry"
- Resolving Conflict
- Being Silent

Calming Down

After an upset, it can be difficult to achieve calm again. Many Montessori preschool classrooms dedicate a corner of the classroom known as the "peace corner." One of its various purposes is to provide a space to calm down.

The space often features some pillows, a carpet, a vase where the peace flower is kept, a calming picture, and rotating items that may include a stress ball, a sand timer or Zen garden. Here, children can regain their sense of calm after an upset.

You could easily implement a similar space in your home. If you do decide to do so, it's best to include your child in the designing and preparation of the space. This way they will feel ownership over the corner, and be more likely to care for and use it.

To create the space together, explain to your child that you are going to create a peace corner. Tell them that one of the purposes of the space will be to provide a place to be when they are upset. In my experience, children can learn to use the space quite well, appreciating it as a short-term refuge when they are upset. Children enjoy crying into the pillows, squeezing the stress ball or raking sand patterns in the mini Zen garden.

Some other strategies for teaching calming down include taking deep, belly breathes, using a stress ball (you can make your own by filling a balloon with flower and then tying it off), or even hitting pillows. Each child may feel differently when they are angry, or may have different responses for different kinds of upsets.

Choose a moment when your child is not upset to present one of the ideas. Practice the concept, and then, when your child is upset, invite him or her to practice one of the strategies. It may take a few upsets, but eventually your child may want to try one of the strategies.

Finally, remember that you are their model. What do you do to calm down when you're upset? That will probably be within their first responses. Try to match your response to what you'd like your child to do.

Being Thankful

Practicing thankfulness or gratefulness has been linked to health benefits and greater levels of happiness. Additionally, it builds and grows relationships, so it's beneficial on at least two levels.

It starts by teaching your child to say "thank you", and ensuring that your child frequently hears you say "thank you." However, you can cultivate thankfulness in your child by engaging in some additional activities such as:

- Writing/coloring "thank you" cards
- Talking about what you enjoyed most about the day before bed
- Making baked goods and giving them away as "thank you" gifts for important people in your child's life (teachers, coaches, grandparents, etc.)

Saying "Please"

Similar to being thankful, saying "please" must be heard frequently so that it makes its way easily into your child's vocabulary and communication habits. Make a point of the importance of saying "please" by providing a lesson shared in many Montessori preschool classrooms.

If you have more than one child, you can do this activity with several of your children. If not, invite friends over or do this lesson as part of a play date. Plan a small snack such as popcorn or apple slices. Invite the children to sit in a circle. Begin passing the plate or bowl around, allowing each child to take a few pieces of popcorn or an apple slice. Have one child hold the plate while the neighbor asks "May I please have a slice?", the child answers "yes" and the other says "thank you."

Children can continue practicing the "please" and "thank you" game until the snack is gone.

Saying "Sorry"

Once again, modeling is one of the best ways to encourage your child to say "sorry." You can place additional emphasis on this by role-playing or talking through situations with your child.

For example, ask your child to play a game with you. Say for example "Let's pretend I step on your foot." Proceed to "step" on your child's foot. Then, perform an exaggerated reaction of surprise and say "I'm sorry." Ask your child to try. Then, talk about how when you hurt someone else and you feel bad about it, it's nice to say "I'm sorry."

Resolving Conflict

In many Montessori preschool classrooms, the peace corner is also a place to resolve conflict. It is here that the peace flower comes into play. This beautiful routine for resolving conflict helps children take turns talking and express their feelings. You can teach your child using the following steps.

1. Show your child the peace flower (can be a silk flower or real). Explain that it is very fragile, like our feelings.
2. Say that sometimes we get angry with each other or with our friends, and that it's normal.
3. Tell your child that when they have a disagreement, they can come to the peace corner.
4. Each person who disagrees has a turn to hold the peace flower. When holding it, they should hold it close to the heart, where we often feel our emotions.
5. The person who is holding the peace flower is allowed to talk. The other person listens.
6. The people who disagree take turns passing the flower back and forth until they can agree on a solution.

Providing a role-play of how this might work is often very helpful. If possible, provide an example of the peace flower conflict resolution process with another adult. Among siblings and friends, this model can work well, and can also be effective for parent-child disagreements in some cases.

Being Silent

Montessori believed that being silent and still was an important skill for children. In the preschool, she taught children the "silence" game in which children tried to be very quiet for as long as possible. The game ends when the teacher whispers the name of each child to line up at the door for the end of the day.

You can encourage your child to practice this art by sitting very still and trying to be silent. Ask your child to listen very carefully to see if they can hear breathing or any movement in their body at all. You may even want to time them to see how long they can last, and encourage them to be quiet for longer and longer periods.

Looking at it today, it seems that Montessori was encouraging a meditation of sorts. The silence game is a time of sitting in the moment, silently reflecting and simply being.

Many parents know that children often decide that they need or want attention at inopportune times. For example, when the phone rings or two adults are having an important conversation. For children who are skilled in silence, a discussion about when silence should be used outside of its meditative purposes can be helpful.

The more children are aware of and the clearer expectations are, the easier it is for them to comply and be respectful. Explain to your child that when you are on the phone or when two adults are talking, that they should practice silence unless there is an emergency. Then, ensure that you immediately attend to your child when you are finished so that their needs are also met.

CHAPTER EIGHT

Conclusion

The Montessori method provides a wonderful philosophy from which to teach children self-care and independence. By breaking each task into small bits, providing demonstrations and hands-on experience, children are engaged and interested while learning. Encouraging children to do more and more on their own meets their innate desire to be independent, and helps them follow their natural path of development.

I hope the contents of this book will be useful to you and your child as you grow together. I say together, because, as most parents know, we learn as much from our children as they learn from us.

Resources

www.montessori.org
www.amshq.org/Montessori-Education
www.montessori.edu/homeschooling.html

N.p., 2016. Web. 30 Sept. 2016.
Center, North and North Center. "Toilet Training The Montessori Way: Tips For Preparation And Success". Montessoritraining.blogspot.com. N.p., 2016. Web. 30 Sept. 2016.
Chitwood, Deb. "How To Help Your Preschooler Help Himself". Living Montessori Now. N.p., 2010. Web. 30 Sept. 2016.
"Inbrief: The Science Of Early Childhood Development". Center on the Developing Child at Harvard University. N.p., 2016. Web. 30 Sept. 2016.
"The Naked Truth On Family Nudity". Parents. N.p., 2016. Web. 30 Sept. 2016.
"Toilet Learning Vs. Toilet Training - Self Development - Daily Montessori". Daily Montessori. N.p., 2014. Web. 30 Sept. 2016.
Tsavliris, Athena. "How To Teach Your Kid Proper Bathroom Habits". Today's Parent. N.p., 2016. Web. 30 Sept. 2016.

About the Author

Rachel Peachey is a Montessori teacher, freelance writer and mom of two little ones. She enjoys living in beautiful Guatemala with her husband and children who were born in 2013 and 2015. She devotes her free time to running a community library she began in 2016 at the local Catholic church.

Visit her website and blog: www.rachelpeachey.com

About the Publishers

Ashley and Mitch Sterling are author/indie-publishers and videobloggers on YouTube known as 'Fly by Family'. When they're not writing or talking to a camera lens, the Sterlings value their time together, in the beautiful bluegrass-laden wilderness of eastern Kentucky, where they live with their two children, Nova and Mars.

Their company, Sterling Production, specializes in producing easy to read guides to help parents get a jump-start on incorporating Montessori inspired learning in their home. These books are created with the busy parent in mind, simplifying their experience with guides that are short and to the point.

Visit our website: www.sterlingproduction.com
Visit our YouTube: www.youtube.com/flybyfamily

Hello,

Thank you for reading 'Montessori at Home Guide: A Short Practical Model to Gently Guide Your 2 to 6-Year-Old Through Learning Self-Care'! We hope you enjoyed this book and would love to hear your honest opinion in the form of a review. Reviews help us to improve our craft and to understand if there is interest in future books like this one. You can leave your review at Amazon.com, on the 'Montessori at Home Guide: A Short Practical Model to Gently Guide Your 2 to 6-Year-Old Through Learning Self-Care' product page, in the 'Customer Reviews' section.

Thanks in advance,

Ashley and Mitch Sterling
Sterling Production

CPSIA information can be obtained
at www.ICGtesting.com
Printed in the USA
LVOW01s1103230117
521855LV00005B/559/P

9 781539 419266